Published by New Spur Publishing

Text © New Spur Publishing 2019

The right of Elliott L. Watson & Patrick O'S
be identified as author of this work has been asserted by them in
accordance with the Copyright, Designs and Patents Act 1988

First published 2019

Websites
www.versushistory.com

Twitter:
@VersusHistory

Instagram:
versushistory

ISBN: 978-1-9996360-6-7

Cover photograph of the University of Washington, Suzzallo Library. Photo by Kallu
https://www.flickr.com/photos/kallu/15311060392/

Dedications

This book is dedicated to you. The potential to write great history is in each and every single one of us – history truly belongs to all. Enjoy it.

A Short Note from the Editors of Versus History

Our mission is simple: we want history students to love history.

As passionate history teachers dedicated to serving our students, we understand the complexities and high level of effort involved in writing a great history essay. We also appreciate the fact that university students really want to produce great responses, but sometimes encounter difficulties along the way. Adding to these difficulties, the prospect of examinations can be very stressful.

For a great many years, we have helped students overcome obstacles to writing successful history essays and, hopefully, within the pages of this book, students around the world can find tips to help them when faced with their own essay-writing challenges.

We aim to 'demystify' the components of a great history essay. We want all students of history to relish the rigours of writing; this becomes much easier to achieve if students are equipped with a range of strategies and techniques to improve their own work, while they work.

We hope that *UNIVERSITY HISTORY ESSAYS AND HOW TO WRITE THEM* helps in some small way with improving your essays. Here's to you and your next great history essay!

Best wishes,

Elliott L. Watson & Patrick O'Shaughnessy

Table of Contents

*****

VERSUS HISTORY

BEFORE YOU START

Before you start...

Before you dive into the tips contained in this book for writing your university history essays, you might find it useful to read the following few pages which give *advice* on issues related to such things as submission, plagiarism, and planning.

Good luck!

Respect the Word Limits

Problem Identified:

"I'm really not sure how much I need to write in my essays. Sometimes I feel I write too much but sometimes I feel like my essays are a little 'underweight'. What do you recommend?"

Recommended Solution:

The first thing to do is to firmly and clearly establish the parameters of the marking criteria/mark scheme. This should be freely available to you from the University and you should not begin researching the essay until you fully understand exactly what is required in order to reach the upper echelons of the mark scheme. Indeed, you should approach your research, planning and writing with this in mind, as this will be beneficial in helping you achieve a higher grade. You need to know what the criteria for success *are* to help guide you towards it. Moreover, you must know what the word limit is and, for essays with a submission deadline (or one to be completed under examination conditions), the time limit. If your word limit is 2500 words, you might well have a 10% cushion – meaning that the maximum limit is actually 2750 words. Whilst this may sound like a significant sum, you will need to carefully marshal your approach to the writing, as you will quickly begin to chip away at that total as you write. You also need to check whether quotes count against this limit. Without the necessary planning, you might end up with an overly long and descriptive introduction which eats away at your word limit and puts you in danger of writing an extended narrative. Perhaps worse still, you could end up going over the prescribed word limit and losing marks. Forewarned is forearmed! You could make a plan before you write, based on the word limit you have been given, as outlined below.

Example in Action:

"What was the primary cause of the French Revolution?" 2500 words

Section	Word Limit
Introduction	*300*
Economic	*600*
Political	*600*
Social	*600*
Judgement/Conclusion	*400*

Sound-off about Submission

Problem Identified:

"How could I let my tutor know how much I enjoyed the course and that I have submitted my essay in a non-sycophantic way?"

Recommended Solution:

Every good tutor delivering a course in a University setting will have a deep-rooted passion for their subject and will have invested heavily in the design and delivery of the course content. In addition, universities around the world have a very keen interest in student satisfaction and engagement; it is in both their professional and business interest to ensure that their students are enjoying the courses on offer to them and are learning. Therefore, one way of letting your tutor know that you have submitted your assignment is to email them directly to inform them (this is in addition to submitting your essay via the designated and appropriate channel, e.g.: Turnitin). To take this to the next level, it is usually best if this process of communication commences prior to the submission of the essay. While there are no specific 'rights and wrongs' in regard to this, it is always good to have open, honest and clear channels of communication with the very people who have set and will grade your assignment. The tips below will hopefully offer a holistic view of tutor/student communications.

Example in Action:

Step	Pre or Post Assignment	Action
1	Pre Assignment	At the beginning of a module, find out the assessment points and begin to harvest key information in relation to this (e.g.: dates, titles, deadlines, etc).
2	Pre Assignment	Informal discussions with Tutor(s)/fellow students about progress, useful study resources, exemplar essays, etc. Perhaps establish support networks if there aren't any in-situ, e.g.: Social Media group.
3	Assignment Set	Commence direct research as soon as possible. Perhaps request that the tutor(s) discuss your initial plan(s) and try to get informal formative feedback.
4	Assignment Set	Submit assignment via designated channels well in advance of the deadline to avoid any potential for late submission.

5	Post Assignment	Email tutor to confirm that assignment has been submitted and with note of thanks for any aspects of help that they have given, in addition to the planning and teaching of the course.
6	Post Assignment	Politely request a follow up discussion to gain formative feedback on your assignment, irrespective of the summative grade. This could yield valuable insight for your future assignment.

Precious about Plagiarism

Problem Identified:

"I am very keen to do well in my study of History and to undertake everything I do with a spirit of academic honesty – my History Department at university has made it clear that any incidents of plagiarism and academic dishonesty will be taken very, very seriously. Do you have any tips for helping me to avoid plagiarism in my work?"

Recommended Solution:

Academic work is the intellectual property of its author(s). Using it without referencing/acknowledgement is a form of intellectual theft. It is therefore clearly unacceptable to use the work and ideas of others in your essays without accurately referencing these at every step. The penalty for doing this is often severe. Different universities have different referencing systems, so you should ensure that you know which system to utilise and apply it consistently throughout. It goes without saying that transparent academic referencing is a core non-negotiable and essential to your success when writing a History essay. However, sometimes students who have every intention of referencing fairly fall into the trap of plagiarising unwittingly, without intending to do so. This is often due to the fact that they take notes from academic books/journals, then forget that the notes they have taken were inspired by or taken verbatim from the work of others. Therefore, one way of ensuring that this pitfall is avoided is to ensure that, during the note taking phase, you cite the full academic credentials of the author/work that you have used. This will help you avoid plagiarism without realising it. You could also use different colour pens/headings for direct quotations and summaries.

Example in Action:

Notes from:
O'Shaughnessy, P. & Watson, E. (2018) Lord Durham; An historical investigation into the contributions of John George Lambton to the British imperial control of Lower and Upper Canada. London: New Spur Publishing.

Summary: Lord Durham was an idiosyncratic member of the British elite during the 1830s.

Quote: "Lord Durham's report into the governance of Canada was a turning point in the history of the British Empire."

An Ode to Organisation

Problem Identified:

"I am usually a pretty organised student – during my pre-U studies, I had a schedule and would divide my time between school work, hobbies, ECA's and relaxation. This worked relatively well, but I wanted to know if there are any other 'life hacks' that I should be aware of when planning for the volume of work on my History degree?"

Recommended Solution:

University courses are a step up in terms of the breadth, depth and sophistication of content and skills that are necessary for success. One major step in the right direction has been outlined already in the 'problem' – organisation. This really does lay the platform for academic development and helps facilitate a good work/life balance. In terms of History courses at university, background and preparatory reading will be critical. History is a rich and stimulating subject in terms of the knowledge and insight required and acquired – reading is the medium through which much of the learning dividends are gained. Therefore, it is a very good idea to undertake some long, medium and short-term planning to help you meet the requirements of the course. The earlier you can start to actively engage with the necessary reading and grapple with the core concepts, the more time you have to begin seriously formulating your essay content and arguments.

Example in Action:

Planning	Potential Examples
Long Term	<ul><li>Collate all the submission deadlines for the academic year.</li><li>Highlight any future potential workload 'pinch-points' in advance so that these can be managed as judiciously and sensibly as possible.</li><li>Source and acquire key texts for essays.</li></ul>
Medium Term	<ul><li>Begin the necessary reading in advance of each essay/assignment that is set.</li><li>Collate exemplar essays and mark schemes.</li><li>Arrange support networks/discussions with tutors before commencing the writing.</li></ul>
Short Term	<ul><li>Prioritise work according to submission deadlines.</li><li>Ensure non-academic requirements/commitments are integrated into your schedule and given priority according to relative importance.</li><li>Schedule time for the assignments that you have been set.</li></ul>

Enter the Ellipse!

Problem Identified:

"Sometimes the quotes that I use in my essay feel excessively long. While this is not always a problem – or a problem in and of itself – when I use a number of quotes in my essay, it can look and read as though too much of my work is the product of other authors, rather than me! What tips do you have to help remedy this?"

Recommended Solution:

Researching the work of academic historians and using quotes to help enrich your essay – where appropriate and to add genuine value – more often than not constitutes a bona fide strength in your work. There is absolutely nothing to be ashamed of there! However, the problem with quotes is often not in the deployment of the quotes – it is the manner in which they are used or in the frequency – or both! Therefore, we recommend that you use quotes for analytical, rather than descriptive purposes; there is a tip in this very book to that effect. However, one way of maximising the impact and effect of the quotes that you use is to ensure that you use just the parts that you deem to add value and augment the argument. The ellipse is an invaluable tool here. Rather than using a long-winded sentence from an academic historian which includes lots of additional and/or non-relevant information, the ellipse allows you to trim the quote so that just the words that are necessary are actually included. It is worth remembering that you are writing the essay for a reader. Readers (generally!) appreciate the point being made in a clear, precise and direct manner. Enter the ellipse!

Example in Action:

Non-Ellipse Version
Lord Durham was a played a significant role in the development of colonial Canada. "Lord Durham had a distinguished career in politics before embarking for Canada as Governor. He played a leading role in the passage of the 1832 Great Reform Act. However, his pièce de résistance was undoubtedly his advocacy for responsible self-government in the Canadas." (O'Shaughnessy & Watson, 2018)

Ellipse
Lord Durham was a played a significant role in the development of colonial Canada. Indeed, it has been argued that Durham's "... pièce de résistance was undoubtedly his advocacy for responsible self-government in the Canadas." (O'Shaughnessy & Watson, 2018) This is validated to a large extent by ...

Use Historiography from leading Historians

Problem Identified:

"I attend all the timetabled lectures and seminars on my course and thoroughly enjoy them. However, I am never sure exactly where to start my research on any given historical topic. What hints or tips could you offer me?"

Recommended Solution:

This is a thoroughly logical and sensible query from any historian at university level. Quite often, students are charged with the study of different historical periods or topics and will be expected to submit assessed work on all of these, which can be quite a challenge in terms of the breadth of knowledge and expertise that is required. However, you will be pleased to learn that help really *is* at hand! For every historical topic that you are expected to study and research, it is very likely that someone else will have written about it at length. It is (generally) only those undertaking postgraduate study that will be expected to encounter and grapple with topics on which there are limited works to consult. Therefore, one way of making things easier on yourself is to consult the works of those who have already trodden the academic path that you are taking. Scholarly discourse is a key feature of the historical community and it is very likely that there will be a community of historians who have written (sometimes extensively) about the topic on which you are working. Find out who the most celebrated historians are, read them, analyse their findings, critique them and quote from them to help you generate an argument/analytical tone in your own essay!

Example in Action:

Step	Action
1	Ask your Tutor which historians have published works on the topic and which are considered/have been considered the leaders in the field through time.
2	Read the works of these historians and take notes on their arguments under the relevant categories (thematic, chronological, etc.) to aid with the essay.
3	Compare and contrast the works of these historians. How has the academic discourse/consensus developed through time? What are the key learning points? What and where are the key quotations that can be used to enhance the arguments that you wish to make? Don't forget to record the full citation credentials and to use the ellipse as and where necessary!

Quote to argue – not to build a narrative

Problem Identified:

"I'm not really sure how to use quotations in my written work, as I haven't needed to do this previously. I feel that I often use quotes as a substitute for my own words. What do I need to be aware of before I use them in a History essay?"

Recommended Solution:

Historiography is fundamental to History as an academic discipline. Therefore, researching the work of academic historians should be viewed as a necessary and enriching prerequisite. The work of academic historians can indeed be used in your essays, as long as their work and quotes are accurately and honestly referenced. Whilst there are no 'hard and fast' rules about what constitutes the 'good' use of quotations in your work, as a rule of thumb, it is usually more effective to deploy direct quotations to help generate/develop/substantiate an argument in your essay, rather than to describe/narrate. Given that you will want to intersperse any quotations with your own words, this approach makes sense as it will help you find a good balance. If you rely overly on the quotes of academic historians to help provide context, background and description, this will end up becoming a dominant feature in your work. Using the quotes of academic historians as a tool to generate and enhance the arguments in the essay is therefore probably a more economical, judicious and effective approach.

Example in Action:

Quotation as Description:

Following the Railways Act of 1993, the first passenger franchise of the railway privatisation process was in 1996. O'Shaughnessy stated that 'By 1997, all passenger railway services had been transferred to the private sector via the franchising process' (O'Shaughnessy, 2018). This proves that the franchising process concluded within 4 years of it starting.

Quotation to develop Analysis:

It has been argued that 'The splitting of passenger railway operations from infrastructure was the critical long term weakness of the privatisation process' (O'Shaughnessy, 2018). Whilst this may reflect … it must be considered that … a counter-argument from the supporters of the privatised railway system is … etc.

Indulge the Exemplars

Problem Identified:

"I am new to University and have heard a lot said about how much more difficult and rigorous historical essay writing is at this level compared to my A-Level History course. I am bit daunted by the prospect and am not exactly sure what the difference in difficulty is. Any suggestions?"

Recommended Solution:

Writing a good history essay is a significant undertaking, of that there can be little doubt. When one factors in the amount of learning, planning, writing and reflection involved in the submission of just a single assignment, it is clear that a sizeable number of hours will have been dedicated to the project. Given this – and the fact that most students strive to be as successful as possible – it is therefore wise to consider what the 'finished product' might look like from those that have gone through the process before. Exemplar essays should ideally include the assignment itself and annotations/comments from the assessor. Not all institutions will make these available, but where they are, it would be wise to consider these at some length. Indeed, these need not necessarily be focused on the exact topic that you will be writing about. Nonetheless, invaluable information can be gleaned. These should enable you to see what actually constitutes bona fide success in a history essay for your institution, incorporate and embed best-practice into your own work, whilst simultaneously learning from the mistakes and oversights of others. Where these are available, use them. Where they are not immediately available, why not enquire and ask? After all, self-efficacy is a positive characteristic and should be actively nurtured by any good academic institution.

Example in Action:

Must haves	Why?
Mark Schemes	To clearly and explicitly outline the criteria required for success/what a successful essay incorporates.
Reading List	This should outline the core baseline reading to enable you to acquire the knowledge/understanding necessary to attack the essay.
Exemplar Essay(s)	These are an excellent resource. Even when exemplars do not address the topic that you will be, they can offer invaluable insight into expectations regarding presentation, structuring, referencing, style, approaches and also the marking by the institution.

Syllabus/Accreditation Weightings	The syllabus should be made available by the institution/History Department for your consultation. This will enable you to see what will be taught, when and how it will be assessed.
Referencing Format	There are many referencing formats; be sure to find out which one(s) are utilised by your History Department.

VERSUS HISTORY

INTRODUCTIONS

Introducing...

Every history essay has a beginning, a middle and an end. We probably all know that. However, everyone needs guidance from time to time about what goes into the introduction. A successful introduction to any essay is fundamental to the success of the essay as a whole. Without one, the entire piece of work is like a house without a foundation.

The tips that you will find in this chapter have been carefully selected to help you overcome some of the key challenges that we have seen occur in the past when students begin writing. We hope that you find at least a few that make a positive difference to your own writing. There were so many that we could have included, so we went with those that we believe will help the most students, in the most frequently occurring scenarios.

Let's jump in.

Tip 1: *Where am I?*

Problem Identified:

"Whenever I write an essay, I never know where to start."

Recommended Solution:

The easiest place to start is with context (or background). Imagine the reader is an intelligent person, but someone who doesn't know the topic you are about to discuss. You must 'situate' the reader inside your essay; inside the time and events that you are analysing. By doing this, the reader will become instantly familiar with their historical surroundings and be immediately comfortable with your grasp of the topic.

To do this, merely address as many of the '5 W's as you can in the first few lines of your introduction: Where? When? What? Who? Why?

Example in Action:

Let's say the question is this:

"How far would you agree that the most significant cause of Hitler's consolidation of power, was the death of President Hindenburg?"

Your essay could start something like this:

When Hitler was given the Chancellorship in January 1933, his position was one of weakness: the Nazis had only three members in the cabinet, they did not have a majority in the Reichstag, and President Hindenburg could remove him at any time. However, within just nineteen months, immediately upon the death of Hindenburg, Hitler had become the undisputed Fuhrer of Germany...

Highlight the '5 W's' in the above introduction

Tip 2: *I Spy*

Problem Identified:

"Whenever I write an introduction, my lecturer tells me I'm not answering the question."

Recommended Solution:

When you first read the essay question you have been given, take a highlighter pen and highlight the key terms that it contains. When you write your introduction, make sure that you address every one of these key terms – exactly as it appears in the question, if necessary. Once you have completed the introduction, take the same highlighter pen and highlight where you have addressed those key terms in your introduction.

Example in Action:

Let's say the question is this:

"How far would you agree that the main outcome of the Soviet invasion of Afghanistan was the collapse of détente?"

Your essay could start something like this:

On the 25th December 1979 a wide-ranging network of Soviet forces entered Afghanistan and set about the systematic invasion of the country. Although the invasion lasted nearly ten years, the outcomes were felt almost immediately. In the years prior to the invasion, the Cold War had experienced a period of détente, whereby the Soviet Union and the USA came closer together and reached a series of agreements on such things as nuclear arms limitations. However, almost as soon as the Soviets crossed the border into Afghanistan, détente began to collapse and the two countries became staunch enemies once more. Although there is an abundance of evidence which agrees with the argument that the main outcome of this invasion was indeed the collapse of détente, it must be noted that there are a number of other...

Tip 3: *Having an Argument*

Problem Identified:

"Is it too early to assert my argument in the introduction? After all, how do I know what it will be until I get into the main body of my essay?"

Recommended Solution:

The solution to this is easy. It's NEVER too early to present your argument. It MUST be stated in the introduction, otherwise the reader will feel unclear as to WHY you are saying WHAT you are saying. Identify WHERE the argument is to be found in the question and get stuck in!

Example in Action:

Let's say the question is this:

"The most significant consequence of the Cultural Revolution was the purging of the CCP". How far do you agree with this statement?

The argument in this question is to be found here:

There were a number of consequences of the Cultural Revolution – literally thousands – but which one was the most significant? The question is asserting that it was "...the purging of the CCP", but it's your responsibility to decide whether this is accurate or not; you MUST argue FOR the statement or AGAINST it.

N.B.
Even if you argue AGAINST it, you must still give it its due importance - you must still analyse and explain why "...the purging of the CCP" is deserving of attention as a consequence of the Cultural Revolution, just that it isn't the "most significant consequence".

...One of the most significant consequences of the Cultural Revolution was indeed the purging of the CCP, as over 70% of the Politburo and 2/3rds of the Party itself were targeted and dismissed – thus centralising even further the authority of Mao. However, regardless of the importance of this, it must be remembered that the initial goal of Mao was to induct the young men and women of China into the revolutionary spirit of Mao's version of communism in order to protect the revolution that he believed was being forgotten by those in power. As a result, placing the future of the revolution in the hands of the young, was a more vital consequence of the Cultural Revolution; far more vital than the purges which, it must be remembered, were nothing new in Communist China.

Tip 4: *Mind Your Language*

Problem Identified:

*"The question often asks, "**How far do I agree…**", but my tutor tells me I shouldn't use personal pronouns such as 'I', 'Me', or 'My' in my answer. How can I say that I agree or do not agree, without using these words?"*

Recommended Solution:

It is always best to avoid personal pronouns in an essay. You need to show ownership of your answer without these clumsy words. If you struggle with avoiding personal pronouns, you could always write your sentence with the 'I' and then simply cross it out (see Example A, below)

Example in Action:

I agree that the most significant reason for the collapse of the Weimar Republic was clearly the Great Depression…

Simply cross out the first three words:

~~I agree that~~ The most significant reason for the collapse of the Weimar Republic was clearly the Great Depression…

This is still assertive and you have implicit ownership of the argument. OR, you can use even more clearly assertive language instead:

***The evidence clearly supports the argument** that the collapse of the Weimar Republic was caused primarily by the Great Depression…*

See? You have asserted and owned the argument, without having to use those words that are simply too basic for a sophisticated essay.

Tip 5: *Present Your Plan*

Problem Identified:

"I am worried that planning each essay in an examination will take too much time and not necessarily result in more marks. Should I ditch planning to save time, or stick with it?"

Recommended Solution:

Planning is a necessary prerequisite for success in any esteemed profession. Lawyers, Pilots, Doctors and CEO's all spend more time planning and reviewing than they actually do 'at the coalface'/'in action'. This should tell you that planning is highly valued. In order to deliver a high scoring essay response, you will have to consider the range of evidence that you will deploy and your overall argument; this is essentially a plan. So stick with it. In fact, you could try this in your university History Exam:

- A. Read each question before starting and reflect on them. Make a mini Mind-Map/Plan for each.
- B. Start with the question you are most comfortable with. Keep adding to your other plans as you go through the exam.
- C. By doing this, you will have the most planning time for the question that you find hardest – a sensible approach.
- D. Faintly 'cross-out' your plans at the end of the exam. The Examiner may well be impressed by the fact that you have clearly planned your answers before starting – which is usually a good sign. **Planning is a Positive!**

Example in Action:

Let's say the question is this: *'The Nazis came to power in 1933 due to the actions of Hitler'. To what extent do you agree?*

You could consider a brief planning format like this:

	For	Against	Judgement
Arguments	Hitler's Speeches. Hitler's 'man of action' persona	Great Depression Political opponents underestimated Hitler.	To some extent because … But other factors such as… also played a role...
Evidence	'Fuhrer over Germany' motto in the 1932 election. Choreographed / stage-managed speeches	6 million unemployed by 1932 Brüning, Von Papen, Von Schleicher failings.	

Tip 6: *Context, Criteria, Judgement*

Problem Identified:

"I need a 'tried and tested' format that I can rely on to help construct introductions to my essays that deliver what the lecturers want. What do you suggest?"

Recommended Solution:

You could adopt a trusted format, such as, **'Context – Criteria – Judgement/Range'**. This should help you save time in examination scenarios, as you will have a fall-back position that does not require a great deal of thought during the exam itself.

Context: Two/three sentences that showcase a command of the topic being discussed: Who/What/Where/When/Why.

Criteria: Define the command terms of the question, upon which the answer will hinge – 'transformation' means marked/radical change.

Judgement: Outline your judgement in relation to the question, with supporting/subsidiary factors that you will also consider.

Example in Action:

Let's say the question is this:

"To what extent did Adolf Hitler transform the Nazi Party in the years 1923-1928?"

Context:
Hitler assumed the leadership of the German Workers Party in 1921, launching the 25 Point Programme which provided the ideological underpinning of the Party… Between '24 and '29, Hitler exhibited the traits of a political pragmatist: steadfastly adhering to his goal of ending democracy while adapting his strategy for doing so. He did this by abandoning violent putsch and adopting democratic means...

Criteria:
In this context, 'transformed' refers to radical change to the fabric of the Nazi Party between 1923-1928, rather than just superficial or short-term alterations...

Judgement:
While Adolf Hitler instigated significant changes to Nazi Party strategy – from 'Putsch' to 'Party Politics' – this does not constitute a genuine 'transformation' as their goal of abolishing democracy remained throughout '23-'28. Changes were made to the governance of the Nazi Party and its finances, but these were of secondary importance.

Tip 7: *Split/Twist the 'Key Words' in the Question*

Problem Identified:

"When answering questions that hinge on **two 'key words'**, *I really struggle with managing the scope of the essay and to generate an argument. For example, the type of question below has the potential to cause me real problems."*

"How accurate is it to say that British trade policy was **consistently successful** *throughout the period 1763-1914?"*

Recommended Solution:

Firstly, do not panic. This type of question does indeed present all candidates with the issue of defining two key 'criteria' words for the judgement – so, you are not alone and are absolutely right to be mindful. However, they also present a realm of analytical possibilities for you to showcase your evaluative/thinking skills. This is how: define each 'key-word' separately, then have some fun playing around with them. Here are just some of the combinations that you could deploy:

> *X was consistently successful to a large/small extent ...*
> *X was consistent, but not successful …*
> *X was successful, but not consistent …*
> *X was consistent, precisely because they were not successful – rather…*
> *X was successful, precisely because they were not consistent, rather they adapted to new circumstances…*

Please note, doing this is not compulsory. Nor is it always advisable. This is just an option for you to consider. If it doesn't empower you – feel free to ignore.

Example in Action:

A recent winner of the University of Cambridge's 'Robson History Prize' wrote a response to the question:

"All style and no substance." How fair is this as an assessment of Disraeli?

The candidate shrewdly used a similar technique, by turning the key words against each other –or rather, reversing them. The response concluded:

For Benjamin Disraeli, style was substance. Therein lies his appeal.

Tip 8: *Don't do That!*

Problem Identified:

*"My essays always end up with red pen all over them saying, **'Don't do that'**, or **'Avoid doing this'**. Can you tell me some obvious Don'ts to avoid?"*

Recommended Solution:

Here's a list of the **Top Ten** things to avoid in a well-structured, controlled, and analytical History essay:

1. Don't use personal pronouns (I, Me, My).

2. Don't generalise. This is a cardinal sin. ALWAYS be specific and use examples to support your points.

3. Don't use contractions. Instead of "*Wouldn't*", use "*Would not*". Anything else is laziness. (We are aware that '*Don't*' is a contraction. Smarty pants)

4. Don't say, "*Some historians argue…*" unless you can name at least one of those historians. Otherwise you sound like someone who is simply 'making it up'.

5. Don't '*sit on the fence'*. Always have an argument; a clear point of view. We don't want to hear that, '*It may be this or it may be that'*. We want to hear a confident assertion.

6. Don't write a sentence that has no relevance to the question. Every single sentence you write should 'service' the question.

7. Don't use language you don't understand. Using a thesaurus to make your work sound 'sophisticated', only draws the reader's attention to words that don't 'fit' in the sentence you have written.

8. Don't refer to your own essay. You should avoid saying things like, "*As already mentioned*", or "*This essay will discuss...*". Doing so makes your essay sound subjective and basic. Don't be self-referential.

9. Don't describe. Anyone can describe something. Your job is to analyse and evaluate its significance in relation to the question.

10. Don't start writing anything until you PLAN. Unless you take time to plan your essay, it will most likely end up a rambling, unfocused mess.

Tip 9: *The Name Drop*

Problem Identified:

"Is putting historiography (the view of an historian) in the introduction a good thing, or is it simply too early? How would I do it?"

Recommended Solution:

It is absolutely NOT too early to start placing historiography in your introduction – in fact, it could be a major help in outlining your argument in relation to the question. Who better to set up your argument than a professional historian!?

Example in Action:

Let's say the question is this:

"How far would you agree that Disraeli's purchase of shares in the Suez Canal in 1875 represented a significant change in British imperial policy?"

Let's say that you agree that the purchase of shares **did** represent a *'significant change'*, then either use a piece of historiography (quote an historian) or **name drop** them:

...if by 'significant change' in imperial policy, we mean that there was a shift away from one based purely upon trade to one that incorporated geopolitical imperatives, then Watson's contention that "... the purchase of shares in the Suez Canal turned imperial policy in an unprecedented direction – towards a more considered view of Britain's role in the world...", is correct.

OR

Let's say that you believe that the purchase of shares **did not** represent a *'significant change'*, then either use a piece of historiography (quote an historian) or **name drop** them:

...if by 'significant change' in imperial policy, we mean that there was a fundamental shift away from the traditional imperatives that drove Empire, then O'Shaughnessy's argument that "... the purchase of shares in the Suez Canal represented no meaningful departure from the way Britain viewed her role in the world...", is infinitely more convincing than that of Watson...

VERSUS HISTORY

MAIN BODY

Making the Main Bit Better

Every history essay has a beginning, a middle and an end. We probably all know that. However, everyone needs guidance from time to time about what goes into the 'meat' of the essay – the middle bit, or the 'main body'. The main body will be the longest part of the essay, so it is crucial that we give good thought to it. The tips that you will find in this chapter have been carefully selected to help you overcome some of the key issues and problems that we have seen occur in the past when students get into the main body of their essays. We hope that you find at least a few that make a positive difference to your own writing.

Tip 10: *Create an Argument Sandwich*

Problem Identified:

"My tutor tells me that my essays are too descriptive and that I need to generate and maintain an argument in relation to the question. I need to move beyond writing a narrative account of events and argue! How do I do that in the body of the essay?"

Recommended Solution:

You can generate an analytical tone by ensuring that the first *and* last sentences of each paragraph provide an argument/judgement in relation to the question. Think of the analytical comments as the 'bread' of a sandwich – wrapped around the evidence and explanation. This will encase the 'story' and the evidence that you can provide in a series of analytical 'lead-ins' and 'lead-outs'. Maintain this approach for each paragraph and every key transition provides an argument, rather than just a story.

Example in Action:

Let's say the question is this:

"To what extent did the British defeat at the Battle of Saratoga in 1777 decide the outcome of the American Revolutionary War by 1783?"

Descriptive Example – Provides story, rather than an argument... Not good:

The Battle of Saratoga in 1777 was an episode in the American Revolutionary War, 1775-1783. The British were led by General Burgoyne and the Patriots were led by Gates and Arnold ... (Candidates Explains the Battle in detail) ... Then the battle ended with over 6000 British troops surrendering. This meant that the British lost this battle.

Analytical 'Lead-in' and 'Lead-out' Example – Each section is 'sandwiched' in analysis... Better!:

The main reason that the British lost the American Revolutionary War by 1783 was the fact that defeat at the Battle of Saratoga in 1777 precipitated direct French intervention on the side of the Patriots. This ultimately sealed the fate of the British forces; 6000 soldiers were taken prisoner ... (Candidate analyses the impact of the defeat at Saratoga in 1777 in relation to the overall defeat in the War by 1783) ... Therefore, the British defeat at Saratoga in 1777 was the key turning point in the War and can therefore be considered the fundamental reason for their eventual defeat by 1783.

Tip 11: *Historiography – Straight to the Source*

Problem Identified:

"When writing essays, I try to support my claims with facts and evidence. However, I would like to 'spice things up a little' with some catchy quotes from historians. What do you suggest?"

Recommended Solution:

The work of historians is the lifeblood of historical discourse and it can provide us with critical insight into the events of the past. In addition, many university textbooks synthesise the work of historians, demonstrating the vital importance of their work. There is no doubting the fact that a relevant, well-placed and punchy quote from a respected academic historian has its place in an essay; it will count as evidence and help build the impression that you have read widely around the topic. You could try to learn a quote (or two) for every key aspect of the syllabus, which you could potentially deploy in an essay. However, you are strongly advised to avoid writing an essay response to 'fit' the quotes that you have remembered – it is highly unlikely to work. Pre-meditating essay responses to include the quotes from historians that you have committed to memory will often result in awkwardly written, off-topic and low-scoring responses. At university level, you should consider the quotes of historians as you would historical evidence; use them only when and if they are relevant to your answer – not just for the sake of doing so. Use them to prove or disprove a point.

Example in Action:

Let's say the question is this:

"To what extent does Khrushchev's Secret Speech in 1956 represent a genuine change in Soviet governance in the years 1917-1985?"

Your essay could go something like this:

In the period 1928-1953, terror was used as a tool for shoring up Stalin's personal powerbase. However, after Stalin's death in 1953, the use of terror became far more discrete and selective. Indeed, Historian Robert Service has claimed that Khrushchev's 1956 'Secret Speech' was the "great turning point of Soviet history …", indicating that there was a paradigm shift in the way that terror was both viewed and utilised after this point ...

Tip 12: *Building Bridges*

Problem Identified:

"I find it difficult to get from one paragraph to another – particularly since I'm moving on to another separate point."

Recommended Solution:

You must remember that there are no **separate** points/paragraphs in your essay – they are ALL connected. All you have to do is build a 'bridge' from one point/paragraph to another. You can build a bridge between ANY two points/paragraphs.

Example in Action:

Let's say that the question is the following:

"How far would you agree that the Domino Theory was the main reason JFK became involved in Vietnam?"

If your previous paragraph relates to an analysis of why the Domino Theory should be considered the main reason for JFK's involvement in Vietnam and your next point relates to the importance of Japan (it honestly doesn't matter), simply do the following:

*Whilst it is clear that the Domino Theory was an overarching and significant reason for US involvement in Vietnam under JFK **(this is merely stating the importance of your previous factor)**, it must be remembered that the theory itself was created as a justification to protect American interests in Asia **(this is your 'bridging' sentence)**. Consequently, the protection of Japan must hold primary significance in comparison to the Domino Theory, if for no other reason than because it was for the protection of US interests in Japan, that the theory was originally proposed **(this is merely stating the importance of your next point...)**.*

Tip 13: *Thinking of a Thematic Approach?*

Problem Identified:

"Sometimes my lecturer says that I need to explore a range of different 'thematic' factors in the body of my essay. I am not really sure what these factors are, or how to approach them. Where do I start?"

Recommended Solution:

Being aware of the 'thematic approach' may be useful when analysing any historical question –particularly **Causes**, **Effects** and **Change/Continuity**. Historians often break down their narratives thematically, so it is definitely an approach that you should be aware of. It might just give you a format to 'fall back on' to help you consider an appropriate range of factors in your essay. The option remains for you to rank these factors in order of relative significance, and/or consider the short/long term implications. Let's imagine that we are discussing the effects of King Henry VIII's 'Break with Rome':

Thematic Category	Explanation
Political	Impacts on government and policy.
Economic	Impacts on finance.
Social	Impacts on society.
Dynastic	Impacts on the ruler/ruling dynasty.
Religious	Impacts on religion.
Cultural	Impacts on societal culture(s).

Example in Action:

Let's say that the question is the following:

"What was the biggest impact of King Henry VIII's 'Break with Rome' in the 16th century?"

Your essay could be organised something like this:

Paragraph 1: *Introduction.* Paragraph 2: *Economic Impacts.* Paragraph 3: *Political Impacts.* Paragraph 4: *Social Impacts.* Paragraph 5: *Conclusion / Judgement*

Tip 14: *Evidence – Make it a Funky Three*

Problem Identified:

"I feel like my essays have a logical, lucid and pretty decent argument as a 'spine'. I follow a 'PEE' paragraph approach. However, my tutor thinks that I could use 'better'/'more' evidence. What could you recommend?"

Recommended Solution:

Your argument needs to rest on the foundations of relevant and accurate evidence. An argument without evidence is not an argument – it's an assertion. You should aim to deploy at least **3 pieces** of relevant, detailed and varied evidence to support your points in each paragraph. The more specific and detailed the evidence, the better. A top lawyer would always aim to support their points in a court with multiple pieces of solid evidence to create an 'incontrovertible case'. You should aspire to do the same.

The 'tried and tested' PEE approach can inhibit your arguments if:

A. The PEE paragraph relies only on a 'single' piece of evidence.
B. The evidence that you use has little relevance to the point made – it has been deployed solely to make the 'PEE' format work, rather than to develop your point and argument.
C. The PEE approach is deployed in a repetitive/mechanical fashion throughout.

Remember that a 'Paragraph Format' should serve **you** and the **argument** … never the other way around. If you are a prisoner to 'PEE', then that needs to change. You might want to consider experimenting with some variations of paragraph formats. A potential alternative is outlined below.

Example in Action:

Letter	What it is ….
P	Point (Make one! Argue it!)
E	Evidence (X3)
A	Analyse (Develop the point)
K	Keep to the Question (Refer back to the Q. Argue!)
L	Link to next Point! (Marry to next paragraph)

Tip 15: *Beat the Clock – Combine Knowledge and Concepts*

Problem Identified:

"I feel swamped by the sheer amount of stuff that I am expected to learn in History. I feel that covering the entire course in my revision spreads my focus too thinly – meaning that when I get an exam question, I don't know enough 'stuff' to write a really detailed answer. However, the exemplar essays are always really long! What do you suggest?"

Recommended Solution:

There certainly is much to learn in History. Historical knowledge is the lifeblood of the historian's trade – so we need to accept that and embrace it. However, you could try revising the 'Knowledge' (e.g.: dates, names, facts, figures, statistics, etc.) that you are required to learn in your syllabus, through the lens of the 'Historical Concepts' (e.g.: Causes, Consequences, Significance, Change, Continuity, etc.) that you may/will be required to demonstrate in your essays. This information is freely available in the Specification for your study programme.

Example in Action:

The syllabus may well give you a clue here – if it states that, for instance, you need to know the: 'Causes and Consequences of the French Revolution 1789-1799', then you know that you should:

- Be able to explain *why* it happened in detail. Know at least 5 short/long term causes in detail – also, why not categorise them thematically?
- Create a fully justified hierarchy of causes in your revision with supporting knowledge – the same would probably be needed for Consequences.
- To go even further, what do academic historians say about the same? You could harvest a few quotes to aid you in your own thinking/writing.

Prepare a mock essay plan once this is completed, to actively apply your knowledge in a manner that is synchronised with the relevant historical concepts. Think about it – if you get an essay in the exam about the causes/effects of this event after undertaking this process, then you will have a rich reserve of prior knowledge and thought to nourish the essay, saving you valuable time in the exam. You never know, you may well find that this helps you to write a clearer, longer and higher-scoring essay. In any event, you will be in an advantageous position vis-à-vis those candidates who have to do all their 'thinking' in the actual exam itself!

Tip 16: *Boomerang Back to the Big Point*

Problem Identified:

"I often find that I just get lost and end up writing lots of description about the topic, rather than focusing on the question. What can I do?"

Recommended Solution:

This problem applies to many students. The first step towards progress is to rethink how you view exam questions. Simply put, this is not an opportunity for you to write *everything* you know. You have been asked a specific question and the examiner only wants an answer to that question. In short, you need to stick to the question. Remember, *'The main thing is to keep the main thing the main thing'.*

Next, ensure that you keep the question in mind. Time is a valuable currency in any exam, so you want to make sure that you are spending it wisely. The bottom line: If you feel like any of the following applies to you…

- A. Waffling around the topic...
- B. Writing a narrative…
- C. Entering into extended description…
- D. Drifting away from the question…
- E. Answering the question that you wish you were asked rather than the one you were asked…

…then STOP and re-check the question. Then REFER DIRECTLY BACK TO THE QUESTION immediately. Self-audit your answer every few minutes; if you are drifting or waffling, then boomerang back to the answer.

Example in Action*:*

Let's say that the question is the following:

"Was Privatisation a success for the customers of the Railways in the period 1994-2005?"

Your essay could go something like this:

…. Privatisation was a relative success for the consumers of the telecommunications industry in the 1980s as it provided a broader range of consumer choice (Candidate self-audits – acknowledges 'drift' away from question focus – snaps back!). Conversely, the decision to separate track infrastructure from train operating companies had little impact on consumer choice after 1994 ...

Tip 17: *Get Connected*

Problem Identified:

"My lecturer keeps on commenting that I need to fully explain each point that I make in more depth and detail. There are lots of frequently occurring comments in the marking, such as 'needs developing', 'add more detail' and 'explain this further'. However, I am at a bit of a loss how to do it. What could you recommend?"

Recommended Solution:

The first thing to remember is that in a timed History essay, you are probably better maintaining a tight focus on a few highly relevant issues and really developing those in depth and detail than trying to discuss so many different points that you end up explaining none really well. Once this is accepted, you are in a position to focus on what really matters – the actual quality of the points that we make. This really starts with good planning before you write, so make sure that you are in command of the facts and have a clear understanding of the purpose and direction of the essay.

One very simple strategy that you can then utilise to ensure that you explain each point in rich detail is to have a bank of connectives at your disposal. When explaining a point, connectives can be used on multiple occasions to really develop both the explanation and analysis. Rather than merely raising a key point and exhausting it in one or two short sentences, the use of connectives can raise both the sophistication and depth of the analysis. You can also use connectives to ensure that you offer multiple pieces of evidence to support each point that you make. There are many to choose from, so here are just a few to act as a catalyst for your own thinking:

Therefore, Moreover, Additionally, Contrastingly, Furthermore, Consequently, However, Nevertheless, Subsequently...

Example in Action:

Hitler harnessed the power of propaganda during the Presidential election campaign of 1932, visiting up to five cities in a day to disseminate his message. Furthermore, Hitler deployed the SA not only to ensure his own personal safety at Party meetings, but also as a tool to disrupt political opponents such as the Communists. Moreover, the SA were presented as a beacon of strength and uniformity against the backdrop of chaos in the streets of Germany …

Tip 18: *The Scheme*

Problem Identified:

"I often feel deflated when I receive the mark for my essay. The tutor will often say that I haven't fulfilled the demands of the question. What does this mean and how can I do this?"

Recommended Solution:

There is an 'easy' fix for this. When I went to university, my lecturer would give us an essay question to answer – with little to no guidance on how to answer it. It was only when I became a teacher/lecturer that I discovered most departments had a set of criteria for students to follow, when writing essays. These are often referred to as 'Mark Schemes', but can also be called, 'Assessment Criteria', 'Level Descriptors', and so on. **FIND YOURS.**

Once you have found the Mark Scheme, highlight the core criteria that you are expected demonstrate. Then, as you are writing, respond to these criteria in every paragraph. *Scheme your way through the essay*.

Example in Action:

Let's say that the University/College wants you to fulfill the following criteria:

A. Important issues relevant to the question are discussed using sustained analysis of the relationships between them.
B. Candidates must demonstrate a sound knowledge of the period.
C. An obvious argument must be sustained throughout the essay, using clear criteria to form judgements with regard to the relative significance of each issue.

Then ask yourself these questions about *every* paragraph you have written:

1. Are my points relevant and have I shown sufficient proof of my knowledge of the period?
2. Are the issues discussed important? How have I demonstrated their importance?
3. Have I analysed the relationships between *all* of the issues discussed? Have I stated their value in relation to one another?
4. How am I judging each issue – against what criteria?
5. Do I have an *argument* and is it shown *throughout* my essay; is it a consistent argument?

VERSUS HISTORY

CONCLUSIONS

Cracking Conclusions

Conclusion paragraphs – sometimes called the Judgement – are a really pivotal ingredient in the recipe of any successful History essay. Given the critical importance of producing a good conclusion, it can be viewed as a difficult and demanding task. While it does require thought and planning, we are certain that a cracking conclusion is totally within your grasp. Moreover, help is at hand! The tips and strategies in this section will hopefully help you see that you can construct a coherent and clear conclusion that competently answers the question. A cracking conclusion does not need to be overly long – nor does it need to be overly complex. We really hope that there are at a few tips in this section that you can readily apply to your conclusions.

Let's get writing a cracking conclusion!

Tip 19: *Hammertime*

Problem Identified:

"My conclusion is always the weakest part of my essay. How do I strengthen it?"

Recommended Solution: Bring the hammer!

The easiest way to remember the functions of the three parts of an essay – the Introduction, the Main Body, and the Conclusion – is this mantra:

Introduction – "Tell them what you're going to tell them."
Main Body – "Tell them."
Conclusion – "Tell them what you've already told them."

Your conclusion should restate what you said your argument *would be* in the Introduction, and what your argument *was* in the Main Body.

Example in Action:

Let's say the question is this:

"*The most significant reason for Henry VIII's 'break from Rome' was his desire to fill England's treasury."*

IF your argument as stated in the introduction went something like this:

...Although the wars with France and skirmishes with Scotland, combined with Henry's overspending, put a burden on the treasury, Henry was never really in danger of bankruptcy. Consequently, attention must be paid to more urgent causes of such an irreparable split between Henry (a staunch catholic) and the Pope. This urgent cause can be found in the desire to secure the Tudor line of succession, rather than the need for money.

Then your conclusion should hammer **the same argument:**

...For much of his reign, Henry was indeed under pressure financially, and the taxes often given by the people of England to Rome would certainly lessen some of this pressure, should they now be paid to Henry. However, it must be remembered that Henry always remained a catholic and broke away from the Pope only because he believed there was no other choice - he needed to secure the Tudor succession by divorcing Catherine of Aragon. He could always raise more money through taxes; he couldn't produce any more children with Catherine.

Tip 20: *Turning the 'Key'*

Problem Identified:

"By the time I reach my conclusion, I have often forgotten where I started."

Recommended Solution:

Very simple – go back to the question and re-address its 'key terms'. 'Turn the Key'.

Example in Action:

Let's say the question is this:

"Britain lost the American colonies because of their failure to understand the terrain on which they were fighting." How far would you agree with this statement?

Your conclusion should directly address (or re-address) the KEY TERMS of the question. Like this:

When Britain finally acknowledged that they had lost the American colonies, they also acknowledged that they had been entirely unprepared to fight on the terrain that they encountered – something Washington and his forces used to their advantage. However, regardless of the terrain upon which the British fought, the more likely culprit for their defeat was the resolve of the 'patriots' to win, what they considered to be, their freedom from tyranny.

Tip 21: *Tell Them What You've Already Told Them*

Problem Identified:

"What should I actually say in my conclusion?"

Recommended Solution:

Tell them what you've already told them**. **Remember the mantra?

Your conclusion should repeat the core elements of the introduction. Your introduction is a summary of what's to come; your conclusion is a summary of what's already been. Don't worry about repeating yourself.

Example in Action:

Let's say the question is this:

"The only real success of the New Deal was that it kept FDR in power." How far would you agree with this evaluation of the New Deal?

Let's say that your introduction went like this:

In 1933, America was in the grip of an unprecedented economic depression, with 18 million unemployed, record bankruptcies, and social upheaval. FDR was elected unanimously in 1933 to remedy these problems, indeed Roosevelt found himself elected, an unheard of, four times. Although his tenure was remarkable in its duration, to assert that this was the only achievement of his New Deal policies – that of retaining power – does a disservice to the many improvements that occurred under his presidency. By 1939, unemployment had been halved, banking had been federally regulated, and relief had been brought to millions.

In your conclusion, simply 'tell them what you've already told them'. Thus:

Clearly one of the key features of FDR's time in office was the longevity of it. However, it must be remembered that he was elected in 1933, when America was deep in the grip of a dangerous depression and was given the task of remedying the problems it caused. The confidence shown by the electorate should be taken as an indicator of his New Deal policies, which addressed the key issues of unemployment, unregulated banking, and the associated social ills of a collapsed economy. Although FDR's presidency in no way solved all problems, to assert that the only achievement of the New Deal was that it helped Roosevelt retain power - does a disservice to the progress witnessed during the Depression.

Tip 22: *Build it Up – Then Knock it Down*

Problem Identified:

"How can I weigh up the factors I have discussed and make sure that the tutor knows which one(s) are the most important in my conclusion?"

Recommended Solution:

You should begin your conclusion by directly addressing the question – after all, we do not want to leave the tutor 'guessing' as to our final opinion on the question. Then, we can deploy an 'age-old' technique used by interviewers when giving feedback to unsuccessful interviewees. Quite often, they will begin by telling the candidate what they found impressive, before delivering the unhappy news, based on the job description:

"Whilst we were really impressed by your enthusiasm, we regret to inform you that on this occasion, we were looking for a candidate with at least 15 years' experience. So therefore, you have been unsuccessful."

You can do something very similar!

1. Deliver your judgement.
2. Outline the 'also-ran'/subsidiary factors of lesser importance.
3. State why the factor(s) that you judge to be more significant are just that – based on criteria.

Example in Action:

Let's say the question is this:

"Was the Assassination of Archduke Franz Ferdinand the main cause of World War One?"

1. The main cause of World War One was the long-term breakdown of the principle of collective security, which precipitated mutual distrust and international antagonism...
2. Whilst the assassination of Archduke Franz Ferdinand sparked hostility in the short term by triggering the conflict between Austria-Hungary and Serbia, it cannot be considered the 'main' cause as it did not ultimately create the context for war on a global scale.
3. On the contrary, the failure of the system of international alliances to prohibit the pre-eminent European powers from entering into direct conflict must be considered as the crucial long-term cause for the conflict, as…

Tip 23: *Assert Yourself*

Problem Identified:

"How do I make sure that the examiner is impressed with my essay?"

Recommended Solution:

Use assertive language to prove control and ownership of the argument and the essay.

Examples:

1) "Clearly the argument put forward is undermined by…"
2) "Although, on the surface, the argument deserves attention, it is not wholly supported by the evidence…"
3) "To claim that this is the most significant outcome is not a convincing position…"

Example in Action:

Let's say the question is this:

"The Weimar Republic was doomed to fail." How far would you agree with this evaluation of Weimar Germany?

Your conclusion could go something like this:

Despite the fact that the Weimar Republic was built on, what many would call, 'unstable foundations', the assertion that it was doomed to fail from its inception, is not supported by the evidence. Clearly, there were weaknesses within the constitution upon which it was based, and it was deeply unpopular to many who saw it as being associated with the loss in World War One, but there is an abundance of evidence to prove that, until the Great Depression struck, the Weimar Republic was under very little threat after 1923…"

NOTE: Being assertive DOES NOT mean being arrogant.

Tip 24: *The Evidence Suggests...*

Problem Identified:

"I always find that I start my conclusion in the same way: 'In conclusion...'. Are there any different ways?"

Recommended Solution:

Use **the evidence**.

Starting your conclusion with the words, '***In conclusion...***' is fine, but VERY basic. There are so many more sophisticated and assertive ways to demonstrate that, **a)** this is a conclusion and, **b)** you have ownership of it.

Don't worry that the lecturer won't recognise your final paragraph for what it is – a conclusion –, if you are confident in the assertive language that you use, then she will be in no doubt.

Remember, the reason you are able to formulate a sophisticated argument throughout your essay is because you have a thorough grasp of the evidence and its meaning in relation to the question. So, why not let the evidence *prove* your conclusion.

Examples in Action:

Your conclusion could start something like this:

Clearly the evidence supports/contradicts the assertion that...
OR

The evidence is overwhelming in its support/contradiction of...
OR

There is no doubt that the argument put forward... is not fully supported by the evidence...
OR

Whilst the argument that... has a degree of validity, there is simply too much evidence in opposition to it...
OR

The majority of evidence tends to agree/disagree that...
OR

Although the argument is reasonably convincing that... there is insufficient evidence to truly support it...

Tip 25: *Check Back for Consistency*

Problem Identified:

"What do you recommend that I do once I have completed the body of the essay and I am ready to write my conclusion? I want to minimise the possibility for errors at this critical stage."

Recommended Solution:

If you haven't done so already, you should check back at the argument that you outlined in the introduction. Ask yourself: Does the argument translate from the introduction to the body of the essay? Does it directly and clearly relate to the question? If not, this is a golden opportunity to correct your work before it is too late. If anything seems vague, or if the connections to your 'main argument' appear implicit or assumed, this is your chance to add a 'bridging' sentence or two to fix the matter. Perhaps add in a direct sentence or two at the end of the 'dubious' sections to make the connection back to the question? Be absolutely sure of the key arguments that you want to put forward in the conclusion. In essence, ask yourself:

A. Does the main argument relate directly to the question?
B. Is it logical and consistent with the general thrust of the essay?
C. How will I justify why this judgement is more valid than an alternative perspective?

Once we have answered these questions, we are ready to proceed and should be immune from the charge of not providing a sound conclusion.

Example in Action:

Let's say the question is this:

"How accurate is it to say that the status of women was transformed under Soviet rule in the years 1917-1985?"

Your conclusion could go something like this:

Overall the degree of change for women in the USSR was mostly experienced in de jure terms, with multiple decrees guaranteeing their equality in law. However, in de facto terms, traditional gender roles prevented a successful transformation in the status of women. Indeed, by 1985 women were still unable to access advanced employment opportunities or abandon domestic responsibilities. Therefore, the status of women was never truly transformed in the USSR.

Tip 26: *The Name Drop, Revisited*

Problem Identified:

"Is putting historiography (the view of an historian) in the conclusion a good thing, or should it only go in the introduction and main body of the essay? How would I do it?"

Recommended Solution:

It is absolutely a GOOD THING to place historiography in your conclusion - in fact, it could be a major help in drawing your argument to a confident close. Who better to help conclude your argument than a professional historian!?

Do you remember how we 'name dropped' in the introduction (Tip 9)? We simply do the same but using different historians or different quotes from the same historians.

Example in Action:

Let's say the question is this:

""The most significant outcome of the Munich Putsch was that it elevated Hitler onto a national platform?"

Let's say that you agree that the *'most significant outcome'* was Hitler's *elevation onto a 'national platform'*, then either use a piece of historiography (quote an historian) or name drop them:

...there appears to be a greater weight of evidence supporting O'Shaughnessy's argument that "... without the Munich Putsch, Adolf Hitler would have remained insignificant and obscure. More than this, the Nazis would have become a mere footnote in German political history...".

OR

Let's say that you **do not** believe that the *'most significant outcome'* was Hitler's elevation onto a *'national platform'*, then either use a piece of historiography (quote an historian) or **name drop** them:

...there appears to be little evidence supporting any claim that the Munich Putsch presented Hitler to a national audience, on the contrary, there is an abundance of evidence to support Watson's view that, "...not long after Munich, most Germans had forgotten the name, 'Adolf Hitler'.

Tip 27: *Exit Strategy*

Problem Identified:

"What's a good way to finish my essay so that the reader is left with the best impression?"

Recommended Solution:

You need an *Exit Strategy*.

The best way to 'exit' your essay is to do so with confidence. How can you do this? *Challenge the question*. If you are feeling confident, take issue with the question; perhaps demonstrate the limitations of it. If you can do this and do it confidently (remember: confidence is NOT arrogance), then you prove that, not only do you have control of your essay, but you have such understanding of the topic that you can actually see *weaknesses* in the question. Do this and your exit from will leave a profound impression.

Pithy: brief, forceful, and meaningful in expression; full of vigour, substance, or meaning.

Example in Action:

Let's say the question is this:

"The foundation for the success of Roosevelt in the years 1933-39 was laid by President Hoover." How far do you agree with this statement?

Please **look carefully** at this question. There are two significant **assumptions** embedded in it:

a) that there was indeed a foundation laid for success at some point;
b) that Roosevelt was successful.

Challenge one or both of these assumptions in the last sentence of your conclusion. Like this:

Although both Roosevelt and Hoover contributed to the policies pursued under the New Deal, neither one could be said to have been particularly 'successful' in tackling the problems of the Great Depression – a point clearly proven by the only real remedy: World War.

OR

In fact, the argument that there was any real foundation laid for the remedying of the ills caused by the Great Depression, is misleading – at best, good ideas were shared between the two presidents; at worst, poor practice was continued.

Concept Check

The final section of this book focuses on the historical 'concepts' that underpin some of the questions you may be asked in essays/examinations. The idea of 'concepts' may sound abstract and even intimidating, but there really isn't much to be worried about – once you have invested some time with getting to grips with them. The advantage of doing this becomes clear when we think of how damaging it can be to misunderstand the conceptual basis of a question; the answer that we supply can be completely misdirected. However, if we understand exactly what we have been asked to do, we are well placed to focus our answer on what is specifically required.

The *Key Concepts* we will explore in this section:

- •Causation
- •Consequence
- •Change
- •Continuity
- •Significance
- •Similarity and Difference

We have aimed to explain these concepts as simply as we can. We really hope that you find it useful and reassuring.

Let's go!

Tip 28: *Causation*

What is it?

History Essays which focus on 'causation' are all about the factors that actually made events happen. Historians are generally very interested in 'why' things happened. They like to know the chronological order of factors that precipitated an event – however, you will need to move beyond a narrative of the 'causal factors' in an essay. You will need to arrive at a 'hierarchy' of causes by justifying which was the most significant.

Suggestions:

A. Stick to a discussion of cause(s) of the event in question – avoid extended discussion of the actual event, or its consequences.

B. Avoid the dreaded 'monocausal' (single-cause) explanation. Historians agree that when things in History happen, they happen for more than one reason. Therefore, discuss more than one reason.

C. Avoid a chronological narrative of factors leading up to the event / occurrence in question. While knowing the chronology of events is always important, you will be asked for an ***analysis of the relative significance*** of one cause in particular or asked to make a judgement which outlines the ***hierarchy of relative-significance*** of the causes in relation to an event.

D. Categorising the causes will help you create a solid argument. You can categorise thematically (economic, political, social, etc.) and/or in terms of chronology (long term causes, short term causes, triggers).

E. Try to add some 'flair' to your discussion of causes by using verbs or nouns into your analysis of causes. For example, instead of *'The Patriots rebelled against British rule in 1775 because of the agitation by the Sons of Liberty…',*

   …you could try something like this:

   'The Sons of Liberty planted the seeds of rebellion against British rule in the 1760s; however, these were inadvertently cultivated by crude British policies that inflamed Patriot discontent, sparking conflict by 1775 …'

Examples of Essay Questions on Causation'

- 'The Hanoverians were invited to take the English throne in 1714 solely because they were Protestant'. To what extent do you agree?
- Why did the British lose the American Revolutionary War by 1783?
- Was the Great Depression the main reason that Hitler became Chancellor in 1933?

Tip 29: *Consequence*

What is it?

Essays which focus on consequences are all about the impact/effects of a given event – it really is that simple! Historians are very interested in the consequences of **key events** in history. For one thing, if an event in history had noteworthy consequences, then the event is probably worthy of study; in other words, it may well be historically significant. However, you will need to move **beyond** a narrative of the consequences in a history essay. In short, you will need to arrive at a *'hierarchy' of consequences* which fully analyses a range, while justifying which was most significant.

Suggestions:

A. You must stick to a discussion of consequences of the event in question - avoid extended discussion of the actual event, or its causes.
B. Avoid an extended discussion of a single consequence of the event. Discuss more than one consequence. Aim for at least three?
C. Avoid a chronological narrative of consequences. While knowing the chronology of the consequences is important, you will be asked for an analysis *and* judgement which outlines the *hierarchy of relative-significance* of the consequences in relation to an event.
D. **Categorising** the consequences will help you create a solid argument: thematically and/or in terms of chronology (long term/short term etc.).
E. Try to add some 'flair' to your discussion of causes by using verbs or nouns into your analysis of causes. For example, instead of *'The main consequence of the Paris Peace Treaty of 1783 was the removal of British forces from the 13 Colonies...',*

> ...you could try something like this:

> *'While the removal of British forces from the 13 Colonies facilitated the official creation of the United States of America, it ultimately laid the platform for a readjustment of British strategic priorities toward the Caribbean...'*

Examples of Essay Questions on Causation:

*   'The main impact of the Hanoverians ascent to take the English throne in 1714 was the consolidation of Protestantism as the primary religion in England'. To what extent do you agree?
*   What was the main consequence of the British loss in the American Revolutionary War by 1783?
*   'The primary effect of Great Depression in Germany was the rise of Hitler to the Chancellorship by 1933.' How far do you agree?

Tip 30: *Change*

What is it?

History Essays which focus on 'change' are all looking for you to determine what, if anything, is different during a specific period of time. More than this, although colleges are looking to see if you can identify those changes, they will also be looking for you to evaluate them too.

Suggestions:

A. Do a **Before and After** check. What was the situation like before, is it in anyway different now?
B. Every question will have a 'thing' that it is being suggested may have experienced some kind of change. Determine what that 'thing' is and then do your **Before and After** check.
C. If you are being asked a question about **change**, then the exam board clearly thinks there is sufficient evidence to suggest there was some. Identify those changes and support your assertions with evidence.
D. **Evaluate** the changes you have identified:
    i.   Judge their significance – how important were the changes?
    ii.   Explain **why** the changes were significant.
    iii.   Rank the changes in order of significance; compare them to one another.
    iv.   Characterise the **nature** of the changes – were they political? Were they economic? Were they social? etc.
    v.   Identify the seriousness of these changes – were they fundamental? Were they structural? etc. This is an opportunity for you to show some flair in the language you use.
    vi.   Identify any **limits** to these changes – were they mostly cosmetic changes? Were they short term? Were they underwhelming? etc. This is another place where you can use flair in your language.
    vii.   DO NOT merely describe the changes – an overly descriptive answer will not gain you the higher marks.

Examples of Essay Questions on Change:

- 'The events of the 1905 'revolution' fundamentally altered the relationship between the Russian government and the Russian people'. To what extent do you agree with this statement?
- How accurate is it to say that Thomas Cromwell oversaw a radical change in Tudor government?
- Roosevelt's New Deal changed the role of the American government in the lives of its citizens. How far would you agree with this?

Tip 31: *Continuity*

What is it?

This 'Key Concept' goes hand-in-hand with another: change. Why? You cannot evaluate what changed unless you also determine what stayed the same. And vice versa. As a result, any question about change will automatically also examine continuity. And vice versa.

Essays which focus on 'continuity' are all looking for you to determine what 'things' remained unchanged and to *evaluate* these 'things' – usually in comparison to what changed.

Suggestions:

A. Do a **Before and After** check. What was the situation like before, is it in anyway the same now?
B. Every question will have a 'thing' that it is being suggested may have experienced some kind of change. Determine what that 'thing' is, and then do your **Before and After** check.
C. If you are being asked a question about **continuity**, then the exam board thinks there is some. Identify those continuities clearly and support your assertions with evidence.
D. **Evaluate** the continuities you have identified:

   i. Judge their significance – how important were the similarities?
   ii. Explain *why* things remained the same and explain the significance of this.
   iii. Compare the continuities to one another BUT also to the changes that took place: were the continuities more significant than the changes?; were there more continuities than changes?
   iv. Characterise the **nature** of the continuities – were they political? Were they economic? Were they social? etc.
   v. DO NOT merely describe the continuities – an overly descriptive answer will not gain you the higher marks.

Examples of Essay Questions on Continuity:

- 'The events of the 1905 'revolution' represented no significant alteration to the relationship between the Russian government and the Russian people'. To what extent do you agree with this statement?
- How accurate is it to say that Thomas Cromwell's contribution to Tudor government was to ensure the continuity of Henry's power?
- Roosevelt's New Deal changed little in the way the American government involved itself in the lives of its citizens. How far would you agree with this?

Tip 32: *Significance*

What is it?

There is no reason to fear an essay that hinges on historical significance. You will probably be required to make a judgement about that significance in a specific period. It is important that you establish strong, consistent criteria to judge significance against. This will act as the compass of the essay, helping you successfully navigate your way. The '5R's' of historical significance are just one framework that you may choose to consider:

- Remarkable
- Remembered
- Resonant
- Resulting in Change
- Revealing

Events in history are usually significant if they resulted in change. You may be asked to consider the extent to which something can be deemed a 'turning point'. This requires that you make a judgement about the degree to which the event precipitated change. Again, you can consider short and long-term change or use thematic criteria to help inform your judgement.

Suggestions:

A. Respect the **entire chronological range** of the question and avoid omitting time. Ensure that you span at least 75% of the period (e.g.: If the question spans 1900-2000, you should cover at least 1900 to 1975).
B. Establish your criteria for **'historical significance'** in the introduction then ensure that your analysis is rooted in that framework throughout.
C. To quickly gauge significance, ask yourself **'If this event never happened, would anything have been different?'**. If the answer – after applying your criteria – is 'no', then that may help shape your thinking. However, sometimes significance is in the **'eye of the beholder'**: just because it is not significant to you does not mean that it has no overall importance.

Examples of Essay Questions on Causation:

- How significant was Khrushchev's 1956 'Secret Speech' in determining the actions of the Soviet Secret police between 1956-1985?
- How significant was the introduction of the longbow in 1290 to the success of the English army between 1290 and 1500?
- To what extent was the Pilgrimage of Grace a 'turning point' in the Tudor period, 1485-1603?

Tip 33: *Similarity and Difference*

What is it?

These two 'Key Concepts' – similarity and difference – go hand-in-hand with one another. Why? It's is very difficult to evaluate what similarities two things have unless you are also able to determine what differences set them apart, and vice versa.

Essays which focus on 'similarity/difference' are all looking for you to determine what elements of a particular 'thing' can be thought of as resembling or being distinct from one another and *evaluate* them as well – usually in comparison to one another.

Suggestions:

A. Do a *similarity/difference check*. Write a list of the elements that resemble one another; write a list of the elements that are clearly different from one another.

B. Every question will have a 'thing' that it is being suggested may have similarities/differences. Determine what this 'thing' is, and then do your *similarity/difference check*.

C. Are there more similarities than differences (or vice versa)? Does this help you form your argument and judgement.

D. Are there any 'Grey Areas'? Are there any issues that have both similarities **AND** differences? Are there **degrees** of similarity/difference?

E. If you are being asked a question about **similarity** and **difference**, then the exam board clearly thinks there is some. Identify those **similarities** and **differences** support with evidence.

F. Evaluate the similarities/differences:
   i. Judge their significance/importance.
   ii. Explain *why* things are similar/different.
   iii. Compare the similarities to one another BUT also to the differences that are evident: are the similarities more significant than the differences?
   iv. Characterise the *nature* of your similarities/differences.
   v. DO NOT merely *describe* the similarities/differences.

Examples of Essay Questions on Causation:

- How similar were the rules of Stalin and Khrushchev?
- To what extent did the rebellions in Upper and Lower Canada have similar causes?
- How far would you agree that the policies of Wolsey and Cromwell were fundamentally different?

A Final Word from the Editors of Versus History

Thank you very much indeed for purchasing and using this book. It means a lot to us as we care about the progress of our readers. Please do get in touch and let us know if we can help you in the future.

Our mission remains simple: we want all History students to really love History; we want them to easily understand how to write better essays. If just one of the tips contained in this book has been of assistance to you in your writing, then we consider that our mission has been successful.

If you found the book useful, you can sign up for updates and extra tips by visiting our website and blog. You can also download and listen to one of our many helpful *Versus History Podcasts* from iTunes and www.versushistory.com.

Thank you for reading. We appreciate it.

Best wishes,

Elliott L. Watson & Patrick O'Shaughnessy

OTHER WORKS BY ELLIOTT L. WATSON, PATRICK O'SHAUGHNESSY AND VERSUS HISTORY

Amazon Bestseller:
33 Easy Ways to Improve Your History Essays

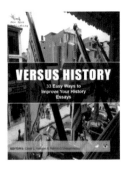

Amazon 'Hot New Release'
Blowing up the Nazis: What you didn't know will blow your mind

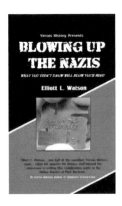

Lord Durham: An historical investigation into the contributions of John George Lambton to the British imperial control of Lower and Upper Canada

*Don't forget our weekly **Versus History Podcast** on iTunes and Spotify!*

AUTHORS

Patrick O'Shaughnessy
Patrick is an experienced Teacher of History at all age and ability levels, with an M.A. (Distinction) from the University of Nottingham. He is internationally recognised as being a preeminent creator and curator of History teaching resources, which he shares via the www.historychappy.com website and his Twitter handle @historychappy. Furthermore, he runs the 'Historychappy Youtube Channel'.

Elliott L. Watson
Elliott has taught History at secondary schools across the world for the last 19 years and has a PhD. He has lectured in International Relations at university level and has published academic articles such as South Asia and the Cold War: Vice President Nixon's forgotten trip to Ceylon (Taylor & Francis). He has his own website offering free resources for students and teachers - www.thecourseworkclub.com - and his Twitter handle is @thelibrarian6.

Websites
www.versushistory.com

Twitter:
@VersusHistory

Instagram:
versushistory

Published by New Spur Publishing

Text © New Spur Publishing 2019

ISBN: 978-1-9996360-6-7

Cover photograph of the University of Washington, Suzzallo Library. Photo by Kallu
https://www.flickr.com/photos/kallu/15311060392/

Printed in Great Britain
by Amazon